Wakefield Press

ô horsey

Christopher Barnett began writing poetry aged 14. He participated deeply in the movement against the Vietnam war; that political commitment has remained.

From the early seventies in Adelaide to France from 1990 to the present, he has conducted writing workshops and continues this work with communities in difficulty. His theatre work is performed in Europe, Australia and Latin America. He and his work have been the subject of French, Swedish and Australian film documentaries.

By the same author

a fist in the face of public taste Experimental Art Foundation 1978

selling ourselves for dinner All Out Ensemble, Adelaide 1982

last days of the world & other texts for theatre Rigmarole Books, Melbourne 1984

last days of the world All Out Ensemble, Sydney 1985

bateu bleu/blue boat, bilingue Edition le Nouveau Commerce, Paris 1994

ulrike meinhof sang Staatsteatern, Stockholm 2003

ulrike meinhof sang Nordiska, Copenhague 2005

when they came/ for you elegies/ of resistance Wakefield Press, Adelaide 2013

ô horsey

CHRISTOPHER BARNETT

Wakefield Press

Wakefield Press
16 Rose Street
Mile End
South Australia 5031
www.wakefieldpress.com.au

First published 2018

Copyright © Christopher Barnett, 2018

All rights reserved. This book is copyright. Apart from any fair dealing for the purposes of private study, research, criticism or review, as permitted under the Copyright Act, no part may be reproduced without written permission. Enquiries should be addressed to the publisher.

Christopher Barnett asserts his right under the Copyright Act to be identified as the author of this work.

Designed and typeset by Annette Hughes

ISBN 978 1 74305 521 2

 A catalogue record for this book is available from the National Library of Australia

 Wakefield Press thanks Coriole Vineyards for their continued support

For
Billy Che Brooks
and
Gary Foley
and
above all,
for her, beloved sister,
La Nga Tai

Introduction

Christopher Barnett's *ô horsey* is at once a work of raw, brutal power and of intense spiritual refinement, as visual and visceral as it is delicate and sensuous. In creating this piece Barnett imaginatively twins a hard-edged contemporary historical understanding with a personal sensibility that gives full due to the body in all its phases and stages. His agonist apprehends the world and his own existence in a language that is by turns spoken plainly, sung movingly and cried in despair. For this poet there is no other choice.

In one mode language may be a kind of machine, a thing of moving parts that – at best – encourages the reader to cool regard, and intellectual analysis. For Christopher Barnett that is not nearly enough. He allows no time or space for intellectual indulgence. For him, language exists as an organism that decays and renews, or perhaps an ocean in which words connect and disconnect, swell and abate. The poet's words bring us to beauty and destruction, hope and its enemies, peace and its dismemberment.

There are many sources for the achievement that is *ô horsey* and a life of study is surely one. The poet has given himself over to the best kind of learning, the tools of craft have been long ago learned – so well learned that they bring no particular attention to themselves but infuse the fabric of the work in the subtlest and most productive of ways. The erudition here simply 'is'. History, philosophy, the learning that comes with a life intensely lived, are marshalled seamlessly to deliver the poem and nothing else.

Inferior poetry strives unashamedly for impact and in so doing aspires to false values. Images are drawn in and arrayed for effect, but ring dissonantly. Rhythm, music, breath, falters or is absent as the words move haltingly or grind to ugly stops. Most obviously, aestheticised language skirts and deflects, resisting the directness of the shared, the tragic experience. But Christopher Barnett here as elsewhere in other of his works arrays symbol, word, image, and aims to see through conventional mists and fogs, spurring the process of understanding, perhaps change itself.

ô horsey presents a distinctive imagining that valorises love and life, yet with full knowledge of the effect on them of our never-ending criminality. We are given a lyric of empathy and regard, set against a quotidian of punishment, loss and suffering. Reflexive virtuosity is absent, the poet has much more serious purposes. Christopher Barnett takes us with him on a pilgrimage into states beyond mere private desire, want, or personal capacity, challenging us instead to face squarely the world's disasters, our own fleshly fragility, and the connections between.

The word 'we' can be a most treacherous reef, but when I read 'we howl/ together/ in terror /of hope's/ hell,' or, 'scarce /we are/ many// in which/ silence shall speak', I understand Christopher speaks again to an intent that has been central to his poetry and his activism since the start. He gives the camaraderie of resistance new dimensions and invites us to join with him – at the very least in the tasks of perception. In powerful, hallucinatory terms he makes the worst that we humans can be and do all too clear. Before anything else, he seems to say, this is how it is – his world, our world.

As countless people have come to sense today, ordinary representation, mimesis, is not nearly enough to capture what we have visited on the natural world and lived through for decades, centuries now. Against this Christopher Barnett offers a corrective in supremely rhythmic poesy whose potent imagery is as urgent as it is so often devastating. He shows all too clearly that what his agonist is living, we are living, where he has arrived, we have arrived.
ô horsey has the visual and intellectual power to draw bonds in words and thought between its creator and whoever is prepared to give themselves over to its flow.

ô horsey is a journey taken in grave communion with the beautiful, black horse of the title. Its teller ranges across a desperate modern history, but also into those stories and beliefs of the people that tell of some force or figure with the power to bind and to loose. We read of 'looking for legba', Papa Legba that is, gatekeeper in Haitian and African cultures, guardian of the crossroads who may halt or wave through whoever find themselves there. Here the poet is not peddling arcana or raiding the stories of others for 'inspiration', but seeks for his creations such agency as might give grace or release.

This work again reminds that Christopher Barnett has long drawn deeply from the world's best creative wells, including that of the Greeks whose myths have afforded a unique way of singing life and the forces that conspire against its survival. The stories of Charon and his ferry, the rivers Lethe and Styx, the trials of Orpheus and Eurydice, so many others, were more than primitive fantasy and never composed with simple amusement in mind. In their profoundly imaginative rendering of war and conquest, of the illogical, the incomprehensible, of the play of dumb fate, the consequences of crossing the mortal order, they served to show the living what they might encounter and have to endure along their paths.

In parts, the work generates a fearful sense of a world closing down. Space and freedom shrink beneath a lowering sky above and a threatening sea ahead – a place in which corporeal boundaries disappear and bodies come to dwell in and with each other, a place where we 'howl in harmony'. As the work tolls the cries of threatened as well as actual loss, the sad truth of what we have done to ourselves and creation down the ages becomes only too apparent again. Against this, the sense of an Underworld ruled by Hades leaps past idle 'myth' to become a profoundly vivid way of conveying the randomness of our fate and disposal.

'. . . sort
souls into sacks
night
luminous
waters
on lake
tall figure
laments
way worlds leave
you alone
you dead
you alive . . .'

If this is our greater history both modern and ancient, it is also the story of cruelty done to the individual body and of our fears as we confront its imminent demise. Thus are we returned to the eternal questions: who will guide me, be with me? where is salvation? what if anything lies beyond? In his search the poet struggles alongside the ebony horse, the 'beautiful/ black beast/ with wings' and all that is in its being, and yet . . . The black horse in Celtic mythology once stood for the strength and maturity to handle what life brings, just as it might be there in the darkest hours. And so Christopher Barnett's magnificent ebony beast – messenger, beloved, companion – becomes entirely apposite to the trajectory of the beautiful cry that is *ô horsey*.

To read this new poem from Christopher Barnett is to be drawn into a tumult of battle for soul, for survival. All the while the sense is one of standing alongside the teller, listening as he proclaims what the edge of life and the threat of the void ahead most utterly feels like. Immense forces are ranged against the small, the human, the chances of victory seem forbidding, but all the while there is also an unyielding effort to wrestle them at least to a halt. The final pages of *ô horsey* arrive with a momentum that is heart-stopping, making them among the most troubling and affecting of all. I unreservedly commend *ô horsey* to readers as poetry of the very highest order.

Angelo Loukakis, 2017

Nantes

Janvier 2016

these
not
notes

from death

bed
ebony horsey

bed
of river

bed
of sea

don't sleep
sleep forever

mélusine
rapunzel
reminds

in this hour

where hours take
all time
they want

memory's
memory

abrasions
in sand blood
& sea
weed

lettres
en lait

left
under shells

hear nothing
nothing
at all
sea rolling towards

you become sea
so easily
ebony horsey

being led
by blind
man i am
not much
more than that

tierisias without
touch for prophecy
if indeed
it was
foretelling

tell
you
now
horsey

as waves
push winds
over our heads

there
are other waves

waves
opening oceans

for friction
of flame

hear
how i howl
horsey
ebony horsey

remembering
orphanage grange
pot holes
way waves
washed each other
like turkish
wrestlers obscene
& sacred

how
i feared
falling in
ô horsey
ebony horsey

i already had

●

ô horsey
ebony horsey

wait
for waves
that come

as
white
on white

walls

•

ô horsey
ebony horsey

these
are not
the words

that made you
wonder wander
in mud

hear heart speaks
without possibility
of solace

souvenance

souvenance
of goat
tied to tree

sees
hears hells
choir call
ô horsey
come ebony horsey

just
down

path

i will walk

with you
horsey it is
too late
now

first
we
fall

climb

bend
to crawl

absence
massacre

memory
breathe
before

body
alphabet

naked
knots

making i

memory
into
memory

suffer

scream

come

suck
saliva

horsey
these not
words

hear
whole
hole

skin
circle
within circle

possessed
possession

once organs
one

carcass
after carcass

birds
mourn
breath

invisible
immolating

horizon

stand
inside black
sun

rejoice

longitudes
latitudes

just
lines

written
with wretched
claws

in chronicle

cry cry horsey
ebony horsey

ô horsey

these not
the words

carnage
comforts
choir

time
troubled
terrified

ô horsey
becomes hardened

marble
or
granite

ghosts
grow own
history here

in hell faint
horsey

go
grieve
on granite platform
washed into sea

fears
can be broken
ebony horsey
heaving hooves
in clay
pits

lithuania
latvia
estonia

body
against
body

sardinespacke
in skin

burning

now

now
this night
horsey

gallop
go

hide
pride
ebony horsey

remember rats rebels
in their cities
inventing path
for plague

plagues
to come

certainly horsey

hear them thudding
from one
corridor to another
looking for arcade

cadavers
cavil certainly

blood
saliva
overflows

ebony horsey devise
drive for death

death
drives

path
after path

with wolves blood
dripping from leaves
as in nursery

rhyme
remembered

desire
to be whispered
to

goat
goes astray
running from rope
to dead
ponies
packed
in quarry

ô horsey
how hard
it is
living lust
after dead

so small
mean
man

made
from
mud

are you refreshed
i am not

sweat steals soul
become sea
of salt
& sulphur

have
to be
humble
in hell

apparitions
enticed
to elaborate

numbers
&
numbers

ebony horsey

calculations
contagious

err
often counting
carcass
after

carcass

tremble
when awakened

horsey hates
humans but does
not envy

stain

émanations
eviscerates

all

tremble

bleed

go

shadows
so many shadows

follow
fallen meditation
amongst murdered

fire

stone
upon stone

reenacting
repentance

turn
to turn

heat humiliates
man in me
ô horsey

man in me
dies

melts
give thanks
i do
not grieve
desire or
covet commemoration

already forgotten

i & i

dance

with
writhing
wraiths

tremble

bring
blood

breathe

body

ô horsey
these not words

arteries
abyss

circle within circle

possessed
présence
carcass after carcass
birds mourn birth

look
for loom

weave
what of wing

âss

pass through

see sea
stretch skin

sea of skin

invisible

end

still

breathe
alphabet

time

serpent sings

time

end

ebony sea

weep

ebony horse
shall drown
in ebony sea

go with goat
live by river

(for ted) a nursery rhyme/for knots

●

where
are words
within this
howling

horsey ô horsey

breath
is all
that

remains

being so
crooked we
are only capable
of constructing
charnel houses

landscape
another

lamentation
little else

can be
erected

before floating
in fields
of flesh

•

horsey ô horsey
ebony horsey

hear holy
hold out
perfect pronouncements
of piety

while we
mangled in mud

pick choose
phrases
out of
past

hear holy howl

perfectly
in tune

parody
of presence

illumination
darkens

with what passes
as alphabet
for them
ceases
to be

but bone
caught in trachea
choking

last breath

last sentence

●

horsey ô horsey
ebony horsey

how my howling
heartens
your
horse's
ecstatic
heart

●

horsey ô horsey
ebony horsey

be black
beautiful black

when wall
white water

comes concealing
choir
of apparitions
clapping
slowest beat

since
fissures formed

death's dance

•

horsey ô horsey
ebony horsey

name
no
names
numbers

numbers
in book
on bed

death drag
east to west

clots of earth
being
turned
over

vanish
vision

carrying us
with current
towards ridge

shelf
shifting

stay
still

in palm
of hands
hurting

beautiful black beast
hurting

cascades come
from centre

but you knew
that

seas seethe
lawless

bring bold
bodies
to surface

here how
slow worlds
go

against granite walls

better being
two twigs

archaic forest
further
down
depths

full
fathom five

plagues arrive
in pairs

vortex visible
where we float
so

so
much
further
down

away from fields
of flesh

beloved black beast

horsey ô horsey

till
tides
beloved

till tides

render winds
heavier in hell

roll

roll

against each other

as
we
fall
further

bound
bound

●

horsey ô horsey
ebony horsey

desperate
to die

birds still
cry to be
heard

live
fully

never
needed
to win

necessity
knew necessity's
noose

noose
in
night

breathe
serpent
into circle

cord
rope

destiny
disguised
as dead
drop

no nights
to trust

here
in hell

just cold
confidence in cold

body become
quarrel

dispute
dismal

here
horses harangue

hour

on end
to end

together
tied to tree

torn
down

further down
into light
so
little

light

night
before i go
to death
bed

voices
can carry

us under

us under

holy
heart of horse

•

horsey ô horsey
ebony horsey

hold on
to me

concentrate
on circles

within whirl
pools
of blood

discharge
here holes
in this
blessed

& beautiful
body

something
like that
threading
through

rivulets
running
down
cheeks

as i confess
to creatures

before beast becomes
judge
jury

surgeon
singing

out oratorio

in such
a théâtre

théâtre
of figurines

effigies

apparitions

looking out window

desolate park

beloved
bring bowl
catch
blood
before it becomes
carpet

you sleep on

shivering

●

horsey ô horsey
ebony horsey

beautiful
black
beloved

break me
me break
break me

droplets
of blood

ebony blood
ebony ocean

why
do you go
to well

why do you
go to well

white water
will wash

you forever
you forever

eternal recurrence
of remains

of remains
wretched
remains

rattling
in closed palms

promise

promise
to throw

ash into abyss
being born

ô beloved black
horsey break

me
down

we been
down
this way
before beginning

ô
yes
me
down

break me down
middle

right
down

middle
maelstrom

eye
eyes

plucked out
on night
barely
remembered

serpent's
suspense

beloved horsey

beloved black horsey

ebony horsey

come with creatures
in clay

red
clay

bloodied
from beginning
beloved

clawed

clawed
coming
out

naked
i know
each inch
of my skin
sister
stone

out into
this

pounding

waters

pounding
waters

waters
cannot
clean

carcasses
carved by claws

come

come

my beloved

black horsey

allow me
to hold

you yearn

these hands

these beautiful hands

●

horsey ô horsey
ebony horsey

how
i remember
her

howl
i remember
her

drifts
so

dear
to me

when precious wind
gone into waters
never coming
back

to her
back

i bent
down

let her
overwhelm
seas within me

let blood
red rain
soak skin

until i surrendered

•

horsey ô horsey
ebony horsey

code
you confirmed
under sheets
of streets
& seas

conducted
your miraculous
caress

calling
demanding
how long
had i died

so she
should sing

to seas
that were
sister

well
welled

up in her
for time
turned by torso

she turns
her
& screams
song

thumped
& threaded
through this
biography without
bitterness

ocean
covered in gates
& doors

murderous dancer
undid
my mystery

nature of numbers

how i wept
only on wings

how i saw
her legs
like

arch
of arcade

body became
lost
so

long
before leap
following
her on
floor of hair
& silk

how long
ô how long
i have been

alive
awake

so
short

sick
since
sigh

sick
since
sight

so they say

so they say
& sing in corridors

wrenched
from whirlpool

sea
of syringes
capsules
fluid
vital

fluid
another

number

number's knots
no

no

dispatch
death from
me beloved
ô horsey horsey

ebony horsey

annihilation's
ambiance

dead
on feet

we dance beloved
ebony beauty

(culture embalmed
floats on froth)

far
from
us

beloved
i'm beaten

but you become
such beautiful
beast

making your way
through
sleep
walkers

sleep
walkers
wielding

fingers
at holy flame

bending over
back

wards
&
wards
of torsos turned
to sleep

when

remember
legs wrapped around
this
thudding
thorax

that can't
tell

whether
it is up

or down

further down

down
in ravines

we take off

our robes
wash each other
in blood

blood washes
clean

condition

call it that
if you wish

so skies
shriek
in this
human field

our skeletons
turn to
melody

you can play
in any temple

adhering
to your arms

beloved
your tongue
teaches

tho
you are
not here
you are here
already widow

mare in mire

cadavers in pyre

let black sun
seethe
beloved

let black sun seethe

who will watch
these words
when morgue
identifies

person
who passed

through

passing
through

singing

ebony horse
sing

from behind
brush

brush my back
beloved
as before

carrying candles
into corridor

drag
me down
into
your
ditch

our bodies
have become wrath

night in night

blood in blood

camarades
will feel
me so cold

beloved
only you
healed by heat

•

horsey ô horsey
ebony horsey

tell me

back to black
back

cheek
to cheek

night's night

atomised
as arrange
my neck
under your arms

frame
of fire

your yearning
from thighs
you turn
& turn
turn into me

climbing coast
of darkness

death's
death

loves

mute
inferno

ash
on lips

soul
grieves
in garden

grâce
unsought
life's

life's
carcass
cherished in charnel
house

go
caress
contours
of her
holiness's

fluid
flow from point

to point
skin never
less squalid

redeems
infinite
contours

fruit's
fruition

so
tired
my body's

teacher horsey
horsey
ô ebony horsey

dream
through
lips
tongue

mouth
swallowing her
from stream

concord
carnal

constitutes
shadow
in night's

fall

amongst
life

less

meant nights
above
all

torment
abandon

when you went
amongst twigs

wraiths
escorted you

as you
tore

down doors
& gates

down so
high star

pass
in mud
sand
my semen
your blood
deep
depths
deep

depth
within

you her
always
come as crystallite

pass
time
fingers through her

hear my
hands
heart
& shape she is
to me
now

tongue
tells instant
after instant

hollow
out heart's
head
into her

horsey horsey
ô ebony horsey

praise
my palms

valleys
sing to
valleys

glorify
going down
into her
come

come
caress us
miraculous

dominion

call shadow's battle

crawl
down
corridor
with cormorants
crying

borrow hell
for breath

veins
viscera
surpass secret
our bodies
share

under beams
bending
to break

believe
blood red
rain

covered in
robe
cloak
of creatures

devour
deep
deep
devours
deep

hear
horsey's
howl

believe
them

rats
relapse
into requiem

this world
is not this
world's

fluid
flows
over
fruit

first

to last

ebony *océan*

run with

rope
& cord

wire

string

between cormorants beaks

sacrifice
skin beloved

in terrible
light

lifting

wrench
whispers
from our loving
tongues winds

hell's hues

odour
of
water

less
oceans
your sex open
with lightness
of tongue

forever
& amen

come
be bird
within me
beloved

come
be beast
within
me my black
beloved

night
another continent

drips
nectar
grief
goes

grief goes
beloved

when your hand
waves flutters
against
this flesh

down
our throats
necks
breast
sex

legs
i weave
into body
to be
bridge

to black sun

float
in you
until

death drives
straight into skin

you sewed
to stop

soul leave

me in centre
of your loving
form

tasted

too

late

always late
death comes
waits
by tree
of pears

flesh
of flesh

flesh's
flesh

legba
loved

loved
in manner
attempted

with her
who follows
river

creatures follow

flesh
of flesh

sculpted
so softly

arms
thrusted
into arms

faith
always fears

•

horsey ô horsey

ebony horsey

in ebony sea

build
blue boat

with broken body
& breath

sing or sail
skin

of ebony
sea
sombre
such hours

barking
at beast

for all
good

it does
no good

at all
inherit illumination
as it

immolates

before

bodies before

bodies

become
being
in purest
sense

salivate

salvation
squandered

down south
of wherever

we are
splitting
skin
with
stone

sea
gulls
pick at scraps
of skin

to cover
surface

ebony endless
sea
soaked in skin

& sound
blessed

blessed
body

whisper
disappear

vanishes

swallow sea
of saliva

mucus

blood

sing
& sing

run
in
ring

sing
& sing

lips
to lips
beloved black beauty

horsey ô horsey

ebony horsey
in ebony sea

•

horsey ô horsey
ebony horsey

horsey
on ebony ocean

horsey
beloved
black horsey
beloved

beauty

collect
bones in bag
go with *grâce*
to garden

stop
at river

wherever you are
close eyes
caress torso
you tore
into

ribbons
flying from cliff

shift
sands
from
vase
let
leavings
vanish

beloved be

by death
bed i lay
still
reading
letter
you gave
to guardian

translating terror
within this
thorax

moment
to
moment
gazing
at granite
of your eyes

watching way
you brought white
robe

hung
it over
painting by person
from 16th
century

sorrow
sewn into silk

tho
covered in thorns

be beast

singing you spoke
so clearly

that morning
not so

long ago
after arriving
by battered boats

on sea
of skin

of skin

you
gave
word

standing
there

staring
like rain
over bed
i lay
truly

broken
broken beloved

& you knew
that better
than any other
leaving
with lamentations

you saw

through black
sun

& its heirs

you came over
carried sheets
from death
bed to window

bed to window

crowd
with horse
crawling along

past us

taking
off turquoise top

cleaning
sheet after sheet

until only rags
littered room

some paper
scribbled

letters
to you
wherever you were

dancing death's duo

getting through

natural

force found us

leg
against leg

hip against hip

robbing wing
from regard

grown

getting used
to annihilation's
absence

came rolling
your body
into me
beloved

horsey ô horsey
ebony horsey

harvesting her
who was in
me

undoing knot
after

knot
night in night
you knew
what it was

i was
doing

devising
diagrams of distance

intimacy

kneeling
we kneeled

neck
to neck

washing with tongue

altered
anatomies

inside
out
we witnessed
each other
from floor

looking out
at space

where we dug
shallow graves
for each other's

heart
when that had
to come
& it came
with each
& every caress

carving
cosmologies
from tears
turning us
like lathe

lovers
we would
become white
wall

hiding history

of how hard
we were
obliged to be

before

before

rains

horsey ô horsey
ebony horsey

beloved
black
beauty

dances
no
doubt

sleeping so
loud

the winter night

we kneel

we kneel

when
fatigued
from flight
into one another's
wings

conceal
our clever secrets
with sweat

saliva

semen

remembering rain
of body
beloved

horsey ô horsey

●

horsey ô horsey
ebony horsey
horsey

ebony océan
pain promises
return
to
every organ

most incision
precision
marks each moment
of night

beloved
side by side

stutter
passion
under or wings
wanton

loved limbs

armed
against assembly

who whisper so
loudly

sun steal
shadow
before our backs
capable
to carve circle
enclosing
elements

so many shadows

birds nest
on head
of beasts

tree
turns

spectres
forget
being
shadow

beloved
within shadow

die
follow
fallen

walk

writhing
wraiths

come

come

light
within
light

tremble

carrying
curse

appalling
assembly
beginning

time begins

before your body

beloved

tides
torrent
of blood

mud

climb
into me

bend
within my body

absence

memory
breathe
before

bind
bound

i do not
shrink before pain
in
any
sphere

love
doesn't make me
small

smaller
than gods
wrapped in chains

running into waters

never
coming back
to commotion

cracks open
sleep

branches break
over body
beloved

waiting
through
so
many
winters

forbearing
bowl & bough

for you
to
come

back
to
back

we taste
one

another

waiting
for that

wind
way it wrenched

vegetation
from viper

mute moon
murderous

perhaps
in that period

you
believe you

loved me
instead

of monument

crowd take
down
down

brick by brick

building
i'd become
home hell
dispelling dark

home
hell wanted
to live
in pilgrimage
before
collapsing

wound rests
for me

to taste

you to taste

we taste
well

of ourselves

of all

organs we cover
as another
robe

to see
us through

these flames

beloved
believing
we preceded

plague
always in premonitions

you shared

as i took
your skin
as scripture
horsey ô horsey
ebony horsey

beloved
black beast

consent
my darling
to darker tasks

asking
you beloved
to never dance

with an angel

•

horsey ô horsey
ebony horsey

horsey
ebony océan

gaze
upon
those eyes

vipers
vigil

speak to
orphan souls
of sea

seeing
gone

shadows

substance

become
being

return
impossible

sombre
earth

clouds smoulder

memory
of your blood

horsey ô horsey

detritus

memories

time
that time
invited

miss
divine

under

agitated waters
sleep heavily

& in
no time

no
time

give
up
écho

interrupted

sense sound
of flame

gather
strength

skins
scorched
presentiment
precise

run
in circles

wear white

on white seas

slipped
over edge

conclusions
concise

beast
followed
by birds

go
to
ground

silhouettes
sacks

carry
weight

of
origin

bodies
orbit at bottom
of *océan*

night
emissary
of ash

watch

absolution
savage

flowers
for time

immémorial
mémorial
living

time
gone

shield

scène
from
seer

run
from rivulets
of blood
on your beautiful
face

torrent
body
territory

divine
dark

night
forever
at furnace

margins
cross

on
way
to
bottom

night
into heart

turn

go
to
it

matter

mouth

magma

water
conquering
time

space
sepulchre

blood
suffocating silence

remembering
annihilation
words
still
words

still
collect leaves
from larynx

exquisité larynx
devour

ash
on lips

souls
go

grieving
go

go
to
lake

caress
contours

infinite
contours

litanies

lamentations

tired

dreaming
thought
mouth

words
routine

solitude
sudden

shadow
before

night
fell

falling

count
days
& night

nights
above
all

dévotion
torment

abandon

pass
from this

to
that

mud
& sand

pass
from this

to
that

time

hear
hands

hollow
out

head

valley
to valley

sing
others

traces

come

come

clear

call out
to other

battle being
shadow

crawl
down
corridor

borrow
breath

beloved

black beauty

horsey ô horsey

•

horsey ô horsey
ebony horsey

how long
ô how long

howl long

howl long

how long

ô howl long
for you
to
for
you
to
breathe air
of my burning

bones
before taking flight

•

how
we howl
horsey ô horsey

how we howl

howl
in harmony

with choir beneath
crevasse

biting through branches

building
a
bridge
with twigs

twigs
between teeth beloved
black beauty
swallowing
soul
whole

what soul
serpent sang
screeching under
growth
of skin
of endless
skin
bone
strontium 90

beloved black beauty
you swallow
soul whole
& sing

how
i
howl for her
night into night
hegel's night
falling

falling
down

how
i howl
beloved

horsey ô horsey

beautiful
beast

biting
bridge into body

once
possessed possession

but you belonged

to heavy water
being trodden
with hooves
so holy
covered in clay

come beloved

wrap wings
& wind around

me wound

opening

opening death's

door mother

called it carefully
observing only
ceiling

she sang
speak simple
son

it is all
coming

down
one
day

deal done

all coming
down one
day

deal done

how she learned
& howled
from legba

certainly
a man

wearing black coat
covered in dust

at bottom
of the world

not so

far from here

holes here
atmosphere under
ground in sea

so many

so many

pale horses driven
mad

when

all hell
broke loose
every year
almost

every week
weak men
tested

strontium
their lack
of sense
or dignity driving
pale horses mad

from one
world
into another

plates shifting
this
way that
way sideways

we laid

ebony beloved
in dark rains

in rains
so thick

we ended
up another

species
stuttering
speeches
to one another

missing

words & sentences
& it didn't matter
at all

matter
matter
matter

how we howl
how long
will we howl

we will howl
endlessly
to beginning
of end

which occurred before
death
bed

lay
the
sheets
of your
skin
over

horsey ô
horsey

lay us down
in death's
bed

here at bottom

beloved black beauty
be beast

for me

trace tongue
along
lines

of
this
body

break it
as a twig

●

horsey ô horsey
ebony horsey

we burst
into blood

& flame
fine
as glass

glowing
in
granite
in heart
of hell

dolente
dolore
heart

fails
falling

evening
of day

writes epitaph
with wind

you alive
he dead

day
dead come

sort
souls into sack

night
luminous
waters
on lake

on lake
tall figure
laments

way worlds leave

you alone
you dead
you alive

a little

difference
diminishes

hour
into hour

wave
after
warped wave

haunt
you into being
still

still

horsey ô horsey

beloved black beast

human husk
pestled in bowl

stamping soul
surely

dolante
dolore

gnarled
bodies
float in bay

lumber
life's fury

nature
knows

night's night

commence
pilgrimage
without purpose
except walking
with galloping
horse

shuffling
slow steps

to grave
where you
cannot be

seen
seen
sun

black
sun

light
so

little

horizon
enters horizon
maralinga 1956
aboriginal community

enter ghost
of flames

a
wake
to all

flinching

forward

foretelling
fall
precisely

inconceivable
immolations

hint
of holy
but none
there for
these of these

only under
seas
bed

having

to hobble
here

betrayed by all
but beast

her

horsey ô horsey

take me back
to beautiful
boulder

read
sourate or *sutra*
crying

from
thorax

heritage
of horizons

holler
throughout
frame

body's frame
black
as beast

horsey ô horsey

beloved black beast

caught between trees
rolling down river

odiously on
& on

blood bursting
into flames

charred child

i am
of human
husk

father
bleeding from mouth
on to ledges
looking out
at forest

mother's tears
wrapping rusted wire
covering window

gazing at gods
coming to her
as dogs

dogs running
under & through
wheels

whining
i still

hear haunting
rubberless
rims

cover road
like cluster bomb

fragment
forever

fearful
of wheels

walk
away from
wheel

into her

ruins

soul
of stones

i am

soul of stones
i am

●

horsey ô horsey
ebony horsey

breathe
for bit

bit
firm in mouth

breathe
a bit

●

horsey ô horsey
ebony horsey

beloved

beautiful
black

beast
hears
her

here
her
howl

hear her howl
into this

husk of man
howling

ache
breath
by breath

hurt
beyond horizon

so
so

little
skin left

stitch my lips
to you beloved

sense me seethe
sense me seethe

spread saliva

across

contours
of our
offering

other

to other

translate
tears
here

with torch

in city
of slaves

now

genealogies
of grief

now
coming so
close

not
so far
from where
i cannot sleep
or
breathe

through this
soul of stones

●

horsey ô horsey
ebony horsey

beloved

beautiful
black
beast

armoured
amorous

all air
erupts
become
enraged beloved

end to end

who witnesses
from throne
of thorns

so stand
still

with sword
book

entrails enveloped
in smoke

deeds
beloved does

proving
her love

luminous

death
disdains

so

so
scorched
search your lips
to wash
with tongue

shiver
shivering

within you

reed
amongst reeds

hear her

hear her
howl

hear her
hail

night's
night

against such
diaphanous
skin

ice's ice

constant

implacable
i in you

implaceable
i in
you in

shadow
infernal

so
it is
sung

throughout
thudding
pages of holy
books

found
in box

deep
in depths

sea bed
dead

flaunts
flames

wheels
continue
to roll
under
water

during thunder

i
inside you
all in one

all
in one

convince crowd
that clings
to cliff
early in morning
moaning
mourn

wrath
washes
me beloved

washing me
beloved

fluids
flowing
from every fragment
of you

hear
throng threaten

ruin
to remnants

roaring

i praying within
your pelvis
pray

rejoicing
in your reign
beloved

horsey ô horsey

beautiful

black

beast
with wings

wrought

with these

beautiful hands
hurting

always hurting

see
she
so solemn

sorting sack
of snakes

on steep
steps

to another

heaven within horse's
horizon

look
for legions
my love

look
for legions
beloved

burnt before
being

element
amongst plenitude
of emptiness

diffused
in sun's

dread drives death

to heart
of matter

powder
of bones

purchase
breath even here
horizon harms
fluid's
firmament

water
on womb's
wing

night
be not
parted

night
be not

parted

•

horsey ô horsey
ebony horsey
beloved

beautiful
black
beast

come
to cage
sea shapes
from shadow
of stones
without souls

sea
sorrow's stone

sea's
memory of moon

ghosts grip
book of birds

wear rags
to worship

hands
tongues
carried in cloth

close
so close
to wound

bodies broken
by fruit

falling

into augustine's hands

exquisite echo
of tombs

birds beat
wings

invincible until infected

hear horsey howl
like locusts

hear horsey howl

sorrow
of sea

surface
of sea
in flame

breath
hammers heart

breath battered
by memory

memory of blood

why
are you writing
in blood
of horses

step
on stones
behind bones

strike
stick against stick

twig against twig

crying
last lasting
crying continually

constant
crying

irreparable

immutable

ineradicable cries

cries
without end

only beginnings

of beginning

maim
memory

horsey ô horsey
ebony horsey

beautiful
black
beast

night heron knows
now in night

in night's night

•

horsey ô horsey
ebony horsey

beloved
beautiful

black
beast

beast take
me turn
me turn
within you

yearn riding
night

mare so black
she is
night herself

fields felt
where

we were borne
under bloody moons

for nothing
other
than
this

landscape
lost
within wave

lost
within you
your sex
still
as stars

history
hides in horizon

see it climbing
stained stairs

wall
of your sex

spark

inflame

shred
within shred

within shred

your
sex still

as stars

horsey ô horsey
ebony horsey

bamboo bending
under back
my beloved

sense stream
of she

singing
so

shrill

your
sex
stripping
skin
from
bones

i am ash
for you
beloved

embers
for you
to wash
into

body
black
beautiful

gripping
tightly
furnace

i am
for you

when
wheels of fire
fall

liberation
of lamentations

howling with
horses

honey

beloved
beast

putting
you into veins

wash
under arms
with your fluid
honey

beloved

bend knees
before your sex
share saliva

contour
into contour

coast to coast
of you

hear her
harmonise with horses
howls

hear her

beloved

beloved be
black

beast
wrapped in arms

always

death's dream
light

limit
limit

how horses
ride

through horizon

ponys
pandemonium

perfect
lust

for

fight

come
come
you cannot

control me
horsey howls within

me here
in her

hear it
honey

hear it
honey

can you
calm down
in depth's
depth

me here
in her

hear her

hear her
here

sea
our solution

•

Nantes

Fevrier 2016

here
her hear

her hear
in humidity

sun's
rains

her reign
her *royaume*

horsey ô horsey

beautiful
black
beast

on heat
beloved

beast takes
all that is

her

body
sponge for souls

mine
down
in valley

between two rivers

between two bodies

powder
of bone

mist

grey mist

watch watcher
with red eyes

follow
night

herons still

in flight
lost
amongst your tears

walls
of tears

dripping
down

prey's prey

meticulous melody

marked
home
in head

clouds
cacophony

force
brothers to bring

sheep
to slaughter
in singular garden

hear her
hear
howl
in harmony

with what
remains of this
body-of-mine

body-of-mine

sweat's
source

horizon
humid

provenance
profound
perhaps

not another
knot

holds you
in her
hear her
howl

blood
in her
blood

down there

down there
in well

weary
as hell's
hot

breath

●

horsey ô horsey
ebony horsey

beloved

beautiful
black
beast

beast take
me turn

hear

hear
her

hold
husk
of what
remains

remains

of this
beautiful body

in you

bird without wing
stone without sting

fall
falling asleep
in your arms

going

down
depths

ground
grâce

into granite

embers in snow
of
contours

of our steps
toward death
learning

how
to
die

●

white wings
ripped

from form

lions take
to beast

horsey ô horsey
ebony horsey

beloved

black
beast

beautiful

numbers
know serpents

who come

who come

to witness

remains
in dark fields
full of flame
& light

odour
omnipresent

man
from man

more bestial
than beast
grove by grove

never yield yearning
beloved

before it breaks

us in us
multitude
in mass

constellations
decomposing
directly after
animals walked

on legs

leg
wrapped around you
beloved lost
within you

lost
within your legs

thigh

thighs threaded
throughout
this

taking you
beloved
from back

taking tongue
into where you
would

conceive

captives

tongue
tasting
every contour
taking you

to another
sphere
in body
we vanish
into one

another

multitude
in sight

night
knows nursery
of night

numbers toll
into one

number

after all

this tongue
circles in you
while you weep
out loud

calling name

my name

almost nothing
after all

animal
of little consequence

small star
in sea
of stars

silent

tuned to tongue

tuned to tongue

turned
within

your
whole
worshipped

so i sing

surpassing all
songs

distances
of distance

corporeal
cloaks
death's desire
darling

beloved
black

beast
beloved

horsey ô horsey
ebony horsey

conceal
captives

collection of captives

beloved
i blister

beloved
i am burning

outside of you

maelstrom
magnificent

monstrous
number without name

so far
within you
stinging
all anatomy
vanishing

ceaseless

creatures come

to tell
of tongue

wrapped inside this whole
of yours
yearning

that

yearning that

i never end

tongue too
eloquent

already opened
gates
of hell

suffocated in sweat

i still

sing

river to river

of her
drawing air
darling

beloved

how
we howl
& roll
in waters

turning
torrents

into one
numberless name

yours
beloved

yearning
in this
hour of hours
for her

will walk
wailing
within her

will moan
until you

can tell
who came
within
you

who
came
within
you

horsey ô horsey
ebony horsey

beautiful

black

beast

solitude
sculpts another
tongue
that can
tell within
you yearning

within you
yearning

equal to eternity

serpent
servant

of this
wretched heart

adoring
another season
of sleep

shiver

sensation
suns sense

shutting eyes
sinless

from that
distance to this

tongue
tasted longitudes
of she

stretching
within

tongue
tasted latitudes

of her

horsey ô horsey

ebony horsey

•

serpent

falls
from
flower

into your palms

circle within circle

sleep stake
in heart

we howl
together
in terror
of hope's
hell

words made way

from another

mouth bleeding

another mouth bleeding

anatomy
becoming abject

object
weak
worship

stand by sea
pass sand
through beautiful fingers
beloved

lead
me to you

such spirits
attend

to
touch

to taste

trace

believe beloved

chains
chanting
in my throat

from thorax

wound

from thorax
wound

take leave
of other

take leave
of other

desire
bent both
our bodies
beloved

beloved
horsey ô horsey

nature
knows
not

this knot
of our body

hovering still
at death's
bed
at bottom
of ocean

seabed sacred
in this
sense covered
in semen
saliva
from our kisses

sweat
from search

returning

return

scarce
we are
many

in which
silence shall speak

sight
tool for tears

sight
tool for tears

equal to eternity

●

I

ô horsey ô horsey
beloved horsey
beautiful
black
beast
i am inside
you yearning
to sing
with your lips
love
of life
without light
without light

birds hauling

heritage of hell

wet

wings
wave after wave

pandemonium
so precise

hurtling
on horizon

pitch perfect

night into night

hearing ghosts howl
gliding
down

so far
down

sound so
hideous

orchestra
of wings

wave after wave

II

going down
further
down

down below

descending

night on knees
hovering
over holes

fluttering

fear fine
so fine

murmur into murmur

abyss answers
after all
quivering
shivering
crying out
in

death's song
ripped from rim
of our being

III

ring
valley after valley

river into river
crevasse after crevasse

ringing
broken bell

ghosts howl
gliding down
down
below

down below

winch flag
up &
down pole

dropped
into deep

earth
& water

hell home
hole

IV

time torn
this torso
this beautiful torso

who
will not weep

air
liquid
gas

flame into flame

stuttering this
always spitting
these words
out of orifice
we wound

wound we are

cities have
every reason
to tremble

arcade to arcade

look at walter
crying cleaning
his spectacles
under smashed store's
jagged window

see through
another season

breathing
it in

language
now
wherever that is

you know
by bag
of bones
she carries

so scorpion said

watch paintings
peel off
skin

simulating serpent

you whimper
you cry

beginning of another
time of another
time

heard
this
& that
when stumbling
& falling

falling over
again
& again

V

ô horsey ô horsey
beloved horsey
beautiful
black
beast
am inside
you yearning
to sing
with your lips
love
of life
without light
without light
with painters
perched on sills

sad birds
seeking salvation

falling
into
fissure

martyrs to moon
being murdered

in ruin
wearing
robe of human
tissue
flesh fabric

drifting

valley to valley

pit to pit

looking for lake

VI

bird's wings
beat
inside skull

as if stones
envelop encephalon

tongue
rope
hanging

from mouth
to mouth
river
ravishing
memory
no

dust

debris
tears

demons just

dread
when watching water

barques broke
path to path

roaming with reptiles

VII

reminded of love
of horse

in horse's hours
slaves sleep

insensate
looking out
to isthmus

praying
for pardon
possessing
only prayer

substance
so specious
screaming
sensible

condemned
crawling to dunes

you yearn

night into night

an affliction
serene sickness

far from
here

horizon hell

fable finished

forgetting

aroma
of ebony

souvenance

sombre

breath by breath

further

down
further

down below

making yourself
smaller
smaller

an art
afforded
such affluence
of minutes
on fuse

learnt
bit by bit

gasp after gasp
going down

to bottom

so close
to ground
most of time

never glancing
at heavens
wherever
they are

ashamed of ascension

horizon hell

counting numbers
knowing

one and one
i & i

bales burning
in fields

clouds come

ô clouds come

come back

up
& down

forever falling
in way

waves do

weeping

weeping then

VIII

ô horsey ô horsey
beloved horsey
beautiful
black
beast
i am inside
you yearning
to sing
with your lips
love
of life
without light
without light

current
controlling
cry

tears torn
torso
tears

contemplating
tree
so tall

opalescent
ornamentation
of orifices

organs

sheets of skin

sails

night knows
horse's hours

glory
& grandeur
ground
into glass

so sharp
making murderous mosaic

cutting cord
horsemen hang

dropping
into ditch

so stones sang

movements of moments
time cannot tell

abjection altered
into affirmation

now
no

rearrange
portraits
& still
lives

still still

place of paintings

still
still

doomed
to do

for damned
birds
hauling

heritage of hell

sound so
hideous

orchestra
of wings

shivering

IX

time torn
this torso
this beautiful torso

who
will not weep

air
liquid
gas

an affliction
serene sickness

horizon hell

aroma
of ebony
souvenance

sombre

breath by breath

minutes
on fuse

horizon hell

weep
weep

cry

tears torn
torso
tears

night knows
horse's hours

murderous mosaic

cut cord

drop
into ditch

stones sang

X

still
still
doomed

damned
birds
break backs bring

heritage of hell

orchestra
of wings

descending

death's song
broken bell
ghost's howl

time torn
this torso
this beautiful torso

moon
murdered

XI

aroma
of ebony

souvenance

weep
as waves do

waves do

weeping

weep

XII

ô horsey ô horsey
beloved horsey
beautiful
black
beast
i am inside
you yearning
to sing
with your lips
love
of life
without light
without light

•

horsey ô horsey

ebony horsey

heart ash

glory
as of old

beauty blesses burnt
souvenance

dust covering choir

annihilation's
intercession

as they sing
in sacred storm

winds grow within
beloved black beauty

flame to come

hear

mostly water
rushing

distance between
tigris & euphrates

only horses
survive here

staying still
so still

roof birds
broke flight

seas become seas

ravens come
flying
with carcass

winds pass
through these hands

these beautiful hands

tears tear
apart ancestors

horsey ô horsey
skin so dark
night knows
black beauty

sailors steal
glance at gold
covered
in slime

we are wire
held together
by breath

series of screams

sorrow in soil

(way water
becomes black)

shifting bones
mound to mound

leaf after leaf

shadows
coming from shadows

waves weeping
maps & men
holding breath

curse of chain

night knows

trees & rope

ash & wind

all fast
to first

kill seed
before growing

sphère dancing

dancing to beating
drum

within wheel
you are

you are turning
back to bone

hearts so hot

you turn

you are turning
to ice

cold coming you

you coming
sweat steals souls
so it is

silhouette
runs through field

weary dead walk
towards figure

you are unable
to calculate

another god
entirely

bird
beloved

in forests
of blood

fruit forgotten
trophy

divine
vines

look for light
gone

between fingers

so scratch soil
for moment

perhaps period long
forgotten

gone
this

gone this world

descend in direction
of insect's wing

horizon just another
précipice

horsey ô horsey
ebony horsey

so still

speak to sea
& orphan souls
listen to memory
of blood

horsey
on hill

wake in water
over head

over mountains
over skies

wake in water

what disappears
illuminates

what appears
darkens

tides tell
how moon
is moved

from heart
to hell

try to sleep
she said

i have not
for all time

living on lip
of volcano

sea
but no light

no light
at all

sea

ferocious heart
tell tomb tale

so souls sing

forget sound
behind you

miraculous beasts

time

obstacle

water
we once were
we once were
water

little more
than that

sweat
& sorrow

tree growing
only in storm

so secret says

night horizon
hell
remember
numbers

witnessing
your life

from far away
in wind
& rain

reckoning's requiem

night
on its knees

night
comes too late

night
on its knees

eat fruit
buried with bones
devour
dancing horse

hear horse
sing
& perish

ash
& absence

blood
& dust

regard
temple of bones
& sand

so it is

scene seen
after eating eyes

memory
has no words

no
no

serpent says
kiss me

serpent
speaks so

softly

slowly

all amazed
at aspect

hear horses
heaving

hear
scorpion speak

light
descends

if it is
light
so sombre

who wails

who

eternity error

it is so

still

sing like serpent

wheel wails

source
sleep

vein to vein

artery
& ash
tremble
in sleep
tremble

see sea
shine

run with rats
& reptiles

to route

taken
by tiller
so speak
to scorpions

spectres
last

love

so
it is

watch wheel

hurl
in hell

speak
to scorpion

suffering so
deep

blood in mouth
makes you murmur

tremble
divine dragged
from one end

to other
skin *sensés*

night on knees

still

time still
so still
so still

horse
walks behind
in rain

& burning leaves
awake in ash

kiss horizon
before
end

hear horsey
ô horsey

ebony horsey

run to sea
with silent birds

drinking
from pool
of blood

memory
maims
such skin

light
from sea
darkens

day ends
days

at end
horsey heaves

tremble

touch
tender ropes

you run

sun
to sky

serpent speaks
so softly

so softly

speak to stones

hear horsey
moan

écho
of waves

hanging
from rope
say goodbye
to horizon

blood
tastes of timber

scream
at bottom
amongst stones
so small
you sought

to possess
possession

curse of chains

cold so cold

so serpents sing

bottom
of bottom

dark garden
grows

ferociously

finally

so serpents sing

teach you
to tremble

tremble

trembling

you turn

time

night
on knees

night knows

hell's horses
here

so
it is

presage of pit

flame
& snow

song of songs

sleep
pities
sleep

horse hobbles

weep
with wind

weep

horizon hell

sing for sea

sing
or speak

you have
no language

or tongue

heal horse
or howl
with her

now

now this
night

this night knows

sing
last songs
inconsolable dead

skin spirit

hear horse howl

vein to vein

horse's hours

fall
& in falling
remember

apple
& grape

veins burn

cruel birds

come

silent

secret

blood bursts
from mouth

sea surges

stones your seeing

stones

your seeing
swamp

serpents sang

breath
into bone

earnest eyes
see

●

horsey ô horsey
ebony horsey

come

crawl
into
cage

confess

confess

confess
only to crows

come contagious
kiss me

beloved
horsey
ô horsey

caw
with crows
covering
every contour
of our
corpses

innocent
as
ice

idol
taken to water
face shore

that is coming

surely
that is coming

choke
chant
in
throat

within circle
only sun sings

sadness
so savage

tearing
out viscera
of all
vital
things

entertained
by emanations

dance
of *disparition*

holy
so
holy

less
leaves
& fruit
insects
eating out
hearts

holy

horsey ô horsey
ebony horsey
we are back
to back

upside
down

insects
incapable
of being

dropped
in glass jars

belong
to me
beloved

beloved
beware

beloved
be within
wall
of you
yearning

grind
down
gates

scripture
suffocating saint
in me

beaten
me beaten
beyond belief

you
mine

maybe
monuments

layer
after layer

ledges
layer
after
layer

vertical

visible

stand
point spectres stand
in line

night
night's

line
after line
alone
angle
after angle

walking with
pebbles in palm

trying out tongue

talk
at apparitions
with words

with

line
so perfect

it makes you
believe

in geometry

horsey ô horsey
ebony horsey

take

take

take

take
my breast

i am

being crude

coarse
clock hangs

from
hung

swinging
with signs

some scripture
surely
density
of birds
disallows
view

vision
of what is

written
less than
memory

now

now
inscribes all
irrevocably

again
being
crude

space
no space

soliloquy
sentence
or two
taken down
from cadaver

crows
cover space
spectres sense
shroud

movement
minute
minimal
night
we shall
not trust

horsey ô horsey
ebony horsey
day

death
comes

stones
arrive as
strangers

silence
orphan

bitter
flags bend

horse's
perfume rest
in veins

possessing
courage of beauty

only one
letter
in annihilated alphabet

miscalculation
in broken abacus

take
my hand

take my hand
take my breath

take
this
breath

birds

breathe

crows converse
while we ride
through bloodied rain

ride

ride

ride
in rains

pure blood pours
on all
you are
in moment

go gallop
a head
i cannot be

crow
collecting

shards
splinters

sea
of my saliva

mourn
morning's
mourning
after mourning

ride

ride

ride
into rains

pure as blood
tearing out
from ocean's
tear

ocean's torn torso
spills on stars

so
sing
so

sing

horsey ô horsey
ebony horsey

soaked in saliva

salts
of supplication

dance with dead

beloved
on walls of falling
shadows
surround cage
too

irradiated idols
meditating with murderers
of moon

bare
foot around your thighs
beloved

too
tired for
silence's
silence

silence's
song of stones

•

I

horsey ô horsey
blessed black horsey

banquet

of ropes

becoming
beast

II

is this
where
it is

souvenance

III

white
sheets
of white

skin sea
sister

skin sea
sister

IV

blind song
sea suffocates

before birds
bite

membrane's
memory

V

voice's
refugee since
thorax threatened
torso
in this
case begins

with lips

VI

moon
malign
metastatic

kite's shadows
shatter
skull

only saliva
sips
from
lips

place
pebble in palm

spasm
to spasm

just so

VII

memorise monument
magma
mud
& man

whomever
he was

learn
longitudes
latitudes
through lamentation

VIII

go
to ghosts

for charity

beg
before graves
brother

crow's
caw never ceases

for condemned
final

station
to
station

horsey ô horsey
blessed horsey
come

quivering

quest
question

able
to annihilate

answers

go down
on grass

grind
face into ground

seal
pores
of skin

filth

fire

arrange
organs ornately
around wheel
with stones

twigs
teeth

crow's
eyes
emerald

evidently

evidently
time

evidently
time to die

hair
falls

chase
concentricus

come
cain

without
white

robe
gloves

white

white

waters

black
as beauty

taste
terre
ene

taste
tears

saturating
skin
& earth

misery
my mistress
so majestic
i drop
to dust

& drop
head into
dirt

strength
not supplication

this
perishing

body passing
through so many
passages

walking
only

amongst
wet
wings

twigs
& tongues

horsey ô horsey
blessed horsey

constellation
clear

so
clear

from
first

bite

trinity
took of horse
's corpse

clear
death
not so
far

from these

cain
come

plant feet
in watery graves

try
to turn

speak softly
to stones

until uttering
for last

time

enters time

gather
miracle

play
peril

skin

bone

haunt

engulfed in flame
taut
torso

light's
trace

sip
saliva
from fountain

blood

saliva

secretions

dead
dissolving

mere matter

shatter

spheres
constellation's

gaze

remembering
under sea
of skin

eat from bowels
of beast

temple
fear constructs

dragons dance
inside skulls

see sea seeing
skull

simple

stone
thrown

number without names

covenants

hear horses

field
in flame

omens

oracles

offal

fall

fall

echo

promise

garments
gathered

sacks of
skin
dance

horses of night
weep
into water

break bell

walk back
into body

see sea seeing
through
horse's eyes

torrents turn
towards
you

breath
bitter

cranium cruel
cavity

walk to well

weep

crawl
concoct cosmologies
crawl

weep
desolate
solutions
uttered
spoken
precept

prayer
come

first
count

cave
in skull

eyes
sense
less

walk
to lake

dead
to world
then

now

then

breathe in

breathe out

barter
memory

elucidate
tears

elegeic
elemental
wish
into being

sad story
wish world
into being

so sad

blood
mucus

writing
on sea

books
of your
being

horsey ô horsey
blessed horsey

sing with serpent

sing

sing

tremble
as i
tremble

ô

howl horse

howl

howl
howl

ô horse
howl

howl
howl horse

howl

howl

scorpion
sings

sing scorpion
sing

ô sing

ô sing

howl

sing

ô

ô

ô

sing

howl
for her

howl
for her
howl
for her

now

now
murder moon
beloved

now
murder moon
beloved

howl
before

howl
before

cruel
birds
come

come

come

•

murmur
in light

leave me

still
wide

awake

emanations
elastic

illuminated
by dreams
dreams of birds
dreaming

blood
in
veins

cadence of corpses
sound so
still

imagine it
her

beating heart
well acquainted
with sea

heat holds
you in hell
flame
follows flame

listen
to form

listen
to leaves
speak

allow body
to become wheel
barrow

cry come cry

be silent
beloved
but sing

place your fingers
in bowl

hell is hell

to hell

terror
harvesting holy fields
here

horsey ô horsey
embrace me

sleep
cannot come

sorrow of stones
halts hearing

except
when you
swim
beloved

spit blood
from mouth

laminate pebbles
you place
in palm

speak
to stone
if you can

true cross
crushed
underfoot

put
twig between teeth

canoes
follow eagle
to horse's skeletons

shadows
sleep in shadow

echo
of extinction

flood fluid

see sea turning
black

ebony

ebony horsey
horsey ô horsey
beloved horsey
blessed

you howl
maelstrom from mouth
known
night's
bones
surround gallows

go

go

go to ground

cover
body in basalt

skin
silent

still

sorrow physics
body
of blood
bone

appetite for apparitions

beloved
ring
broken bell
in hell

stars
moon
perish

stroll
in seaweed
regard brother's head
gaze at you
go

skin of night
knot

laugh
with legba
believe in birds

waving his stick
within
wind

trample
over twigs

tremble before
history

trembles

turn
sea to sea

●

papa legba
weep

for wanting

weep
not only
for him
& other

come
want
whole

course

story
of snow
still

unfinished

hollow history
out

breathe on me

go
down

go

become breath

sound

whisper

heart

speak now
of her

skin's delirium

want her
présence

appearing
& disappearing

know knife

amulet
memory

here

speak
to her

caught in circles

begin
to walk

here
in half
light

silence
of your breath

breathing

you breath breathing

cut contours
in silence

secret
of sea

this
time
takes

now
or later

ghosts
melodies

wrap
gut

of goat
around ourselves

destitute
erudition
menace
milk white

horsey ô horsey

howling

contour
of body's
chains

remember

waves
black as beauty

focus
on fluid
& flame

time
to miss
that
time gone

cover
body in flood

howl

this hour

skin
sky

blind
sun

weeping's
weight

come close

burn end
on end

revolver
at temple

whisper
under breath
light
houses hell

open up
to ravens

hear them hear
see seams
unravel ripped
by ravens
without

remorse

forget

shallows

depths

drive you
forwards
& down wards

out
in open

hunted
haunted

encircled

eviscerated

wonder
as children do

how deep
is the deep

let sun sleep
know by knot

dance

pity
simulacrum
water
wraith

body in song

see skin
of our bones

see skin
shatter

slaves

look
on your faces

remembering

pierced
earth
packed
with fossilised
millions

murmur

remember

time enters time

surrender

witness
wait
wait

oracle's
ordeal

fortify
hell

numbers
prologue

time
over

become blind

as stones

do
damned dialogue

clamouring
in corridors

sleep dreams

body only
trinity

trinity torment

hit rock
bottom

sublime
wound

stains

●

Nantes

Mars 2016

horsey ô horsey
beloved horsey

hold blade
between teeth

as we trot
to charnel

towers
at top
of mountain

looking for legba

he will hear
her

he will hear
her

come

comes
towards us
with wooden cane
& battered book
of his longing

he calls
up wind

to welcome
whites of eyes

so
still

so still

speaks
to us
only in song

terrible song
telling

telling all
in split
second

we will
wash our limbs
in heavy water

legba
tears out page
after page

batter boats
bearing words

we cannot

bear
weight of water

oceans will open
legba leans

on rock
planted

in depth's
depth

path
plea

for time
to enter time

legba laughs
all his teeth
knives
we know

knives we know

from days
disappearance

vanishing
point to point

shake tree
on shore

so it's sound
can carry me

me it can't

because it bleeds

rustling requiem
but it
is all
stillness

legba looks

horsey ô horsey
dances in waves
waves weeping
for her

waves weeping
for her

flowing from
wound

arms
healed by excavation
with utterly useless
tools

syringes
& straps

cord

rope
made for
my neck

know
knot
perfectly

except
mouth full
of seeds

present for papa
legba

whose presence
palpably
enter
& departs

so i also

lay wreaths
on water

for all luck
it will bring

no luck
at all

legba learnt
that long time
away in another
time

space
we steal
to remember

it all

we remember
it all

it all

it all
night
into
night
no

mercy

horsey ô horsey
beloved horsey

legba
brings bag

for me
to carry

to crowd crying
in complete
encirclement

you can
just hear
their calls
their crying

but it is
their waving arms
& shaking legs

that brings
it to
your attention

come now
learn how
to cry

with worlds
we are

with worlds
we are

run
into
deeper
water

beloved horsey
run into deeper
water

cover wounds
with water

run

run

capture
& cage night

•

dream dream
dream no more
of the dead

dream no more

horsey ô horsey
beloved horsey
ebony horsey

taking steps
syringe in arms
held aloft

wanting
to hold you
close

in dream
that comes
no more

clean as cloth
in charnel house

howling out

horsey ô horsey
beloved horsey

blades
shining

even in night
night

shining

starless skies
press face
against window
watching you

horsey ô horsey
beloved horsey
blessed horsey

galloping
over graves

so close

ocean
so close

you can hear
waves push
towards whatever i
remains

deepest waters

depth's
depth

so close

face pressing
against window

disfiguring

tears
that come

ô tears
come

almost
endlessly

horsey ô horsey
blessed horsey

darkness
has eyes
gazes back

at ragged thing
i have become
we mighty we

no man no
but every bit
a man
made for monuments

legba laughed
ô legba laughed

man
monument

clay
in
beginning

marble
in end

one step
away

this blood
of mine
doesn't dry

flows
fluid

magma
from
man

outside
it rains
blood red

blood
red

morning
in mali

legba listens

stroking
my cheek

tasting tears

legba listening
before it comes
falling from
horizon

to tear
one all
of us
apart

shade
even in shadow

night illuminates
almost all

faustus
forgot that

being mind
less

cage closes
in

quite quickly
cardiologist called
out to crows
resting on sill
looking in

being bird
attached
to wires

going

circle
into circle

rapidly

have undressed
for so many
this month

except for her

horsey ô horsey
beloved horsey
ebony horsey

bite
into me
beloved

no harm
can be done

that has
not been done

ten thousand things

haunt
& hunt

haunt
& hunt

hearing her
howling

& ocean
weeping

her weeping

ocean howling

so close
it is
so it is

horsey ô horsey
beloved horsey
blessed

galloping
over graves

dance
death devises

choreographed
through canals
of my heart

howling

for her

can

i be

clearer

concise

night
illuminates

night's
age begun

beginning

bite
your way
through me
beloved

care little
beloved
blood
cannot congeal

beloved horsey
ô horsey

bite
your way
through me

obliterate
sound of ocean

weeping

howling heals

•

horsey ô horsey
beloved horsey

here hear
we weep

ebony horsey
blessed horsey

go blind

end(s) of world

pulling close
together too close
for comfort
colliding

birds of prey
gathering

turn
gaze

share
with shadows

walk down aisle
remember faces
bodies
& souls
annotations in atlas

we wound

weeping

we weep waves
tidal & terrible

tear apart

count days
going down
so slow

measure
pace
& pressure
to decimal point

collect
fishermen's bones
prepare funeral pyre

sing another song

quiet
& quivering
in corner

immune
inhale ice

worn
down to bone

forget route

veins still
washed
down

howl hoarsely

make out
word or two

fall to bottom
of sea

fall

breath by breath

cover eyes

close mouth

debased desdemona
demanding deal

mind
& heart
equal constituents
in chemistry
poured down sink
so

so just

just so

who has name

who has number

another circle

break down
into bits

ash
& bone

pulled from grave
some solitary day

feet touching
soil
or sea
everything else evaporates

run away
with horsemen
when they come
to gates

pull bucket
from well

overwhelmed by omens

seek guidance
to see you
through passages

hide behind hedge

between us bridges

never come back

mouth
full of rope

endless
sleepwalking

charnel house
still continuing
at this hour

know numbers

sleep
under bodies
in pit

stay there
wait
weep

●

night not
day not

day knot
night night
day disappeared

vanished

vanished with vigils

that distinct

possibility
i do
not live
with possibility

matter pure matter
engels wrote eagerly
to karl that
matter

horsey ô horsey
beloved horsey
ebony horsey

here
in here

without question
here

here her howl
my beautiful beloved

horsey ô horsey

negation
of negation

horsey ô horsey

quantitative
to qualitative

horsey ô horsey

unity
of opposites

horsey ô horsey

iron laws
legba listens

tapping cane
into clay

tapping

gazing

tapping

iron laws
he hears
quite clearly
from my blood
stained mouth

iron laws

horsey ô horsey
hears so pain
stakingly

so still

i here her

i hear her

weep for wound
we bear

we haul

we

•

horsey ô horsey

howling so harsh
vigorous & rigorous
beloved ebony horsey

overpowering others
her who wonder
if i
more wind
than man

witnesses
sharing tears

shadows themselves
becoming isolated
forgotten

as all
collect
within
these veins
of mine

of mine
uncertain
in this hour

camarades cher camarades
chase birds
disappear

suffocate

death being
long night
many

decades dead
it seems

yet so
beautiful
a body
still

ferocious
fixed for fight
with any
movement

steps
as always
understated
until knife goes
in

& in

is that clear

better be
before you take
breath

even under

these circumstances
am i clear

stay still
horsey ô horsey
beloved

speaking
slowly to others

whom wander
in & out with clip

boards

names & numbers
long since learned
by heart
this bad
longing heart

all day
night now

cover you
with black sheets

for whom
were you
waiting
sister

waiting
at well
with
eagles circling

birds
not benefactors

sieges
in hell

formidable force
of fluid
passes within

praise
tongue

envoy comes
to convert

poised
with poison
sister

shelter
meridians

throw
light

come
late

fact
fears

here
& now

panic of pulse
remembering

vocabulary
of vipers

come

come
into corridor

break
down bird's
wing

way you have
with beasts
& martyrs

we are slaves
sister

to movement

smoulder
sister

stay
still

speak

trials
& trails

see us
slither

time into time

hour
into hours

call
birds bring
in time

we walk
within

here
& there

spectre still

time
enters time

gaze
with eyes
closed

far away
fabric thread

first
to last

tap hard
today

desecrated water
exalts

estranged
& subdued

pass
through

haunts women
who wait
hewing
hieroglyphs

heart
contrite

lost

bearings

direction

forgive flight

what
of wing

need nectar

now

howls
heard before
felt

wear veil
learn ceremony
when allure gone
& fervour
begins

fall
down
sister

debrief *démon*
only to apprehend
dance

ballet
barbarian believe
in night
of night

hour of hours

sleep inevitable
spéculation
stand vigil
with vipers

gesture
forgotten

after all

vanish

•

holy horsey
ô horsey
how we howl

howl

soon

enough

in dark

immaculate
intersection

slaughter
house comes

soon
enough

come

wait
for proposition

body
guards broken
song

composed
in consolation

circles
within circles

currents

swim down
détour

in garments
i gave you
sister

calculate
carefully

exterior
interior

you
comfortable

niche
or knot

archimedes
expected

apparition

pilgrims
perhaps

weep
& fall

seam
sewn

fall

on knees

remember
exact details

place
& purpose

ancestral
self stained

be
my twin
sister

reverberate
in room

count

shot
again
& again

breath
less

heresy
here time
burning

gift
of going

walk down
descend

with velocity
of vermin

past
out of past

symmetry
solved

vision
precise

in veins

veins to veins

neglect
needs nectar
now

heal
hour

ô horsey howl
for me beloved
ebony horsey

survive sorrow
from fibre

minutes
or hours
rival

be calm
sister

stop

trembling

find thread

cover spectrum
of spectres
who come
to sing
an old song

continue to carry
curse

communion
with cargo

stress
so subtle
seek companion

remember this

scale
of terror

forgive song
for secret
it sings

weep
longitudes
& latitudes

fall

hell's heritage here
hear near
heart of harbour

righteous
run
& ring bells
for birds

remember

head nothing
no
knot

noise
lace

days
disease

heals heirs

but you
obliterated

morning
obstacle

cease

ablaze
apparitions

cry
in

ceremony
of remembering

call arteries

clogged
but still

torrential

beloved horsey
excavate elsewhere

with enemies

watch water
spill
from source
beloved

●

secret

stone

details *incommensurable*

twigs tell
that

congo
zaïre
what
ever

they want

& they want
everything

rubber
diamonds

soil
sand
& stones

whatever
can be
wrenched
from mouth
of earth

from depths

you cannot see

sea remembering

whoever we were

we are

créatures
so cruel

leave

leave us alone
in night

night knows

wind's will
overpowering
incessant

alive
in midst
of fire

storm

invade
every orifice
open

murmurs
in light

leave me

still
so still

dream
of birds
dreaming

forever falling

heat holds
you in hell

flame
form

cold
so cold

what did

you want
beloved

science

times
enter time

cry please cry
before breaking

conceal
chorus
in horse's
heart

weep

learn from leaves

sleep
cannot come

perhaps
in next
knot

hear
heat heave
it's way

towards you

beloved
ebony horse

night illuminates
no

sorrow of stones

sorrow of stones

sustains
only survival

that can be
weighed
with wings

damnation
as always
decisive

• *Hopital Nord Laënnec Nantes*

I

learn to howl
in harmony
horsey ô horsey
beloved ebony
horsey

deliver us

deliver us

under
pass
to shaft

turn
tourniquet
tighter tighter

until
trembling
you are trembling
trembling

until trembling tells
task

wash come clean

II

horsey
holds head
on your shoulders

blind

fatigued
by foretelling

oracles

remember sound
bodies being
dragged in ditch
100 years ago
10 years ago
1 year ago
afar

tal afar
clogs your veins

so too
haditha

too many towns

i will name
every one

until your body
bends into unconnected
circles

torn in tension

torn
i will tell you
towns will be
written all over
cadaver that
my wish

III

what
is weight
of water

in this
hour

in body

in body
of oceans

IV

feel form
of palsy

as you touch
surface of sea

V

sense science
terribly

wrong

VI

beloved

narrate nightly
disaster

until unseen
consciousness

let levees break

one
after
another

choice
cancels circle

engel elaborate

wrapping thread
around his fingers

while sketching
decisive diagrams

he
is to be
trusted
above all

men

VII

syringes scenes
past path station

of cross
hair of rapunzel
souvenance steals
second within

second
you know
story

her hair
attic

prénom révolutionnaire
présent

dans le calendrier
républicain

witch

il se fête
de le frimaire

we know

how it went
went with wind
& dead
leaves

beloved

bathes in dead
leaves

odour
of
ecstatic

that makes
you

forget facts
do
not
forget

facts

VIII

remember

remember how

remember howling

remember how

memory pass
through walls

of your skull

IX

silence
seems possible

only in voice

of strangers

X

air
house of horizon

walk
back
so far

you slip
into lake
of silver

you
you will not
want to pass

night here

night right
here

in any
case

come with candles

there

will be
mourning

when
when

when horsey

walks on water

• *Hopital Nord Laënnec Nantes*

heirs remember
earth
feminine

horsey
masters

heartbeat

heirs of horsey
remember
empire
noose

around our necks

common
as any
partisan
in pripyet
marsh

hurl
embodiments
& effigies

into hole
gouged
with claws
& a gaze
branches
eaves
cannot conceal

arrows
in flesh

grieve
ground
in sleep

come

to crater

circle within
circle

water blood
& dust

abraham
holds heir
high

sea
string
of saliva

falls

falls
from
lips

dead son
dust
break at bottom

of seas
beloved

aequinoctium

sounds
breath & beats
body makes
moving through circles
tears
another

river

go
to gallows

depths within depth

last

instant
final

hideous hands
wave in air

water
ô
water

wait

beloved

emaciated
& empty
wraiths watch

for feast
of flesh

come
with crew
& claws

soul's subjugation

hear horses
tremble

swallowing stones

remember

go back

distance to distance

forest
secret

part days
with desire
death

count
age heavy

odour
of birds

war

deep in dream
i ran
& ran
into i & i
knew some

time ago
ago

go

run
into fruit
of sorrow

words
wind

windows
wind
man

sew rough garments
from eagle's wings

or go

naked
dreaming
words

alphabets
earth
breathed
vows

words
wind

beating door
windows

bread of tears
wind

song flame's death

sing to someone

beloved

they are all

breaking
apart
easily as equations

wash
water

bathe
in blood
& basil

bury being
urgently

it is
so cold this day

all the others

shroud
shrinks through
the clouds

word
man
died
with

rain

until end

earth's
end

piss
on stained soil
beloved

& bite me
maybe
to marrow

• *Hopital Nord Laënnec Nantes*

I

house
of ruin

halted her
beloved horsey

horsey ô horsey

she imagined
shelter of she
wolf

II

live
presences trembling perfect
with your enemies
beloved

she

seeks them out
with sheaf
& blade

time
not for living

horsey
with honoured heart

bridled
the bitch
in dark

enemies
enunciate

with weight
of heavens

III

depart
with seeds
& crow

crows
still

captivate

IV

her mouth
meadow

fields of flesh
feeding forest

animals
before annihilation

water
hums under
ground

so surface
never still

captives
comprehend curse

clearly
do you

do you

comprehend curse

speak softly
if you can

such small space
between terror
& truth

V

she slave
come with beloved
to bloody water.

come
with claw
& chains

no knot
now kneel

bury
body in bamboo
reeds

reed
i will play
saddest music
strengthening
skin so
dry you know
you are close

to death's temper

VI

drink my blood
darling

let it drip
down

your beautiful lips

VII

kiss blade
beloved

sharp

severe

certain
it cuts

precisely

honour
hewed with absence

of hesitation

horsey ô horsey

ebony horsey

beloved horsey

VIII

it will come

no surprise

colour of condition

black so black

it is
beautiful blue
& grey
of most
turbulent

oceans

IX

time

flight

flow
of blood

mucus
brain
matter
vital

juices

only she wolfs
sip

sated

only when soil
covered in scraps
of skin

pray

for poisoned horses

you heirs
of interminable
horror
pierced by beauty
of liberation

X

know
enemy's
neck

know

map

of their matter

living matter
living souls

reproach
those who run
with gaze

that will
finish families
heritages
futures
darkest clouds

covered
with light

imprinted
on walls
pavements
other
persons

that's clear enough
companion read
wilfred burchett

account of falling
time on trachea
for example backs

heads
on fire
all this
& that

horsey knows

she has always
known

bleeding
burning

blood
burns
like oil

• *Hopital Nord Laënnec Nantes*

path
perishing

beautiful
black

horsey ô horsey
beloved horsey
ebony horsey

beloved
beside me
beloved
beside me

collecting
twigs

transform
into totems

beloved
be black

always
suns stop

over her

light no
light

drums
beat

no beat

bring birch
beloved

carry
all with creatures

through woods
to funeral
dance
anguish
in her heart
laying down on dead
leaves

darkness
delirium death
devises
for you shadows

torment
too docile
a word

fatigue
teaches me

to sing
alone at night

or in celebration
of the calf

tears,
pass

walk barefoot
with beloved

gallop on
and die
route lamented
only
once

learn
from linden
tree

remember
each branch

listen

fall
amongst dead stars

sing
so close
to birch

near basin

path
turns
& turning
turns

grasp my grief
for a moment
mourn
now for neighing
horses

edge on edge

breathe

sing

it is
time
entering time

soon
moon
shall strike
me across face

that i should

be beyond
loving

horsey ô horsey
beloved
blessed horsey

ebony horsey

your four
great limbs

cage & captivate

• *Hopital Nord Laënnec Nantes*

it is so
dark so dark

it is so

horsey ô horsey
beloved horsey
ebony horsey
blessed

blessed
do not weep
when i bite

into your flanks

do not weep
hear me weeping

love
of my horsey
i bite

into her flanks
crying

crying out
that
which I

can barely give

word to
tonight

this night

i disrobe

gazing at her
how she gallops

horsey ô horsey
beloved black horsey
ebony horsey

weep i weep

•

falling

falling
into each other

horsey ô horsey
beloved horsey

whole

blessed horsey
black

clouds come

concealing horizon

horizon howls
from hell
to here
hear

listen
as legba
does

to doomed

to damned

soil surrenders
so

easily

so easily
species
lay on earth
from here

to hell

hell
whole

horsey ô horsey
beloved horsey

observed orifices
of dying
& dead

dead's
triumphal torrents

take face
from
you yearning
for body
not so
separated from skin

feeling fibre
cloth clinging

so sombre skin

euphoric carcasses

worm way
to apple

alchemy arranges all
& nothing

horizon hell
horsey ô horsey
beloved horsey

celebrate collapse

lay
in lavender

ignoble
ignorant

essence
not element

here in hell
cortège comes

again
& again

grovelling in gravel
taking trail
through sand
to skulls
embedded in escarpment

devotion deranged

current will churn
cavalcade

one moment
or another

washing away wave

affronts amnesia
kicking
in masks

in face

in teeth

pools of
tears

cry please
cry

before
breaking down

all together now
in chorus

end close

such specific
detail
scars
signs

moment
menace
& messiah

whatever comes first
cloud come
ô clouds come

night
an ocean

saviour cannot swim
except escorted
by eels

swimming in sleep

seventeen enigmas

number
night knows

from beast
before barrage
went down

down below

down below

lay down

in lavender

sweat speaks
grandeur gone

remedy
ruin

not equal
to task

stained skull

amulet
desired in deluge

wave into wave
come
come
close so close
to shore

horsey ô horsey
beloved horsey

blessed horsey
ebony horsey

carcasses
cover surface

skin
sheet north

west

south

east
skin sheet
sea
skin

sea of skin

suffering of sea
shadow of sea

here in hell
horse

no secret
who hides
in wind
who taught
you terror
skin to skin
surface below surface

horizon hell

night knows

fall remains

frightening

death diligent
tomb tells

death not deliverance

resurrection rigmarole
rise & rise

again & again
tiring task

fatigued forever

walls of cave
world

walls of cave
you
are
drawn

horsey ô horsey
beloved horsey

come

come
clouds come

come with condemned

leaves

skulls rotting
fruit

dissolves in night
ancient night

arena
of absent
present

still
so still

ruins reign here
in hell

carbon dioxide
urine

faeces

sweat

not so solid

go glorify
fluids

go

fluids flow
into river

remains
bones so many
bones

territories

built on bones

dead weeping
in confines
of their traces

trace
touch

trace
touch

skin to skin

sea to sea

bridges of bones
bone
bones be bitter

bones be bitter

living souls

consumed for cotton
cloth

worn
while
laying in lavender

surrounded by skulls
of someone's sons

tear
tissue human
tissue stains sea

skin to skin

wound we are

we are repugnant

tears
in heart
tearing tissue

human tissue
here
& there

innocent immaculate i&i
whomever
we were
see sentinels

night knows
night knows

torment taught
dancing

so close

so close
to sea

ô sea

memory of sea

man
made of mud

murdered
whole
dominions disappeared

tongues
torn from mouths

languages lost hanging
from trees

here in hell

death light weight
for family tree
then & now

then & now

haunted hunt here

clouds come
ô clouds come

contemplate
man in morsels

so it is
it is so

drape
dreams in death

nothing noble
barbarism
became being

rains heavy
torrents

mud made
men

slipping species

slipping
into sea
of mud

slip
into sea

slip
into sea

●

Nantes

Avril 2016

horsey ô horsey
beloved horsey
blessed
ebony horsey

tied by cord
under your stomach

dragged over
granite

blood
leaves

trail
words

cannot comprehend
how low
horizon
is
to
hell

•

horsey ô horsey
beloved horsey
ebony horsey

still

here
hearing breath
break

into words
or
wind

beloved horsey
still holding syringes
between teeth
as bit

for me
to use
going

under
under

•

horsey ô horsey
beloved horsey
ebony horsey
still

here hearing breath

break
into words

or winds wrapping
around body

stooping
to
collect
coins

clean
wth
saliva

count
by burnt book
i carry
everywhere

draped
in
blood
surgeons
stained
father's
shirt
robe of flesh

worn to walk
through mist

poor
& dying
pretend
to be prince
of all

dominions

•

horsey ô horsey
beloved horsey
ebony horsey
still

here
hearing breath
break
into words

wandering
amongst waste

seas
of saliva
sperm sweat
surtout sang

cloak
i wear
over
robe
of
flesh

skin
of mine
shedding

through which
words whistled
between lips

love
trying
to love

camouflaged
for condemned

walk into winds

night knows
what's been
let loose

sands smeared blood
blackens

cut
away now

fever form
tied in tourniquet

nightmare
remember
everything

exactly
trembling

you are
trembling

hunted
&
burnt

twirl twigs
in palm

bring bodies
over fields

understood
ultimatum

sing
whose skin
sorrow

such sheets
of skin

spread wings
shadowed
by sea

soil
& blood
mud

embracing
skin

hanging from
bones

turn around

& turn
to thorns

horsemen
heading horses
towards tower

lethal longing

beloved
disappearing
in last
instant

truth so taut

final
blow

horse's eyes
so exquisite

breath into breath
beneath breath

veins
time

betray testament
before barrage

ask no favours

consolation

contempt

conclusions
start
for another
vanishing
point

messengers
arrive
defecate while dancing

ancestors absolute

sequence
of steps

kneel
cross yourself
take in
tongue
& tell

pauses
in path

shout

shred
salvation

weight
of water
keeping you
under

keeping you
from
singing
that song

in empty rooms

vulnérable
vain

sense
stupor of shadows

memory of horses
halts you

beware
of beast
bringing
you back

secrets conceal
sound of souls

come
to crater

witness
wind

gaze
at gates

sheets
of wind

you once wore

breathing space
spellbind
death
with
tumult of tears

remember
burning
horse's
heat

●

Acknowledgements

It has an enormous signifcation, for me, that Angelo Loukakis, a writer and a man I deeply respect, has written the forward to this volume.

I thank Michael Bollen of Wakefield Press for his continuing support for the work.

I thank Geoffrey Datson and Annette Hughes for their collaboration in this publishing project. They mean more to me than words can give breath to so I hope the breath between words – my epenthesis – express my love & respect.

I thank the very great musicians in Nantes, who have joined me in concerts, Scott Stroud on banjo, Will Guthrie on drums & percussion and my constant companion in work Laurent Berthomier.

I thank my collaborator, Stephane Anizon of Le Dernier Spectateur and remember my fiercest collaborator who died in 2010, French film maker & German writer, Thomas Harlan, who for many decades enriched my work with his breath.

Christopher Barnett
Mars 8, 2017, Nantes

Wakefield Press is an independent publishing and
distribution company based in Adelaide, South Australia.
We love good stories and publish beautiful books.
To see our full range of books, please visit our website at
wakefieldpress.com.au
where all titles are available for purchase.
To keep up with our latest releases, news and events,
subscribe to our monthly newsletter.

Find us!

Facebook: facebook.com/wakefield.press
Twitter: twitter.com/wakefieldpress
Instagram: instagram.com/wakefieldpress

www.ingramcontent.com/pod-product-compliance
Lightning Source LLC
Chambersburg PA
CBHW031801220426
43662CB00007B/481